Choosing
LIFE

Choosing
LIFE

POEMS OF DARKNESS AND LIGHT

JOHN SIECKHAUS

To order additional copies of this book, contact:
Xlibris
1-888-795-4274
www.Xlibris.com
Orders@Xlibris.com
702355

Contents

4

5

6

7

For my wife, Ann

ABOUT THE AUTHOR

John Sieckhaus was born in St. Louis, MO and educated in Catholic schools, eventually earning a Ph.D. in chemistry at St. Louis University. The seminal moment in his young life was the slaying of his parents by his by his paternal grandfather, and his subsequent suicide, events which propelled him onto a life course dictated primarily by his responses to this tragedy, his own errant choices and the acculturations of family, church and society. He married his wife Ann in 1963 and they are parents of three children, Lisa, John and Michael. By the time he was 30, he was living the *American Dream* with a loving family, a successful career and a house in the suburbs when depression became a steadily increasing reality in his life. Resort to hospitalization, psychotherapy and chemical dis-ease management proved to be a mere palliative in a desperate striving to arrest the pain, and it was only through an encounter with the living God through the support of a small Christian community that his journey of faith, remembrance and healing could begin. As a scientist involved in the development of weapons systems his conscience eventually led him to challenge his company's involvement with nerve gas research and he resigned his position. With each step in his vocational journey, from teaching environmental chemistry and ethics courses at local universities, to forming his own environmental consulting firm, to working on the development and financing of non-profit organizations, the healing went deeper until he was gifted with a revelation of his family pathology which provided clues concerning his own responses to life.

His memoir entitled *Inching Toward Heaven's Door, A Would-Be Alchemist's Journey of Faith, Remembrance and Healing* was published in 2001, his second book, *Chemicals, Human Health and the Environment, A Guide to the Development and Control of Chemical and Energy Technology* in 2009. The poems contained herein were written during the 20+ year period from 1994 to 2015 and many reflect aspects of his healing journey.

1

HOMO SAPIENS

How suddenly the seed
comes to bloom,
that germ of angst
bursting through
the psyche's shield
to bring all manner
of outrageousness
to the fore,
a confounding sense
of shadow and light,
bane and blessing,
futility and purpose.

Creation's voice
fell uneasily
on this hominid line,
born as it was
in explosive chaos,
strained from primeval soup,
nurtured through
countless sublimations to
overcome baser instincts,
called to be joyous with the
rules of the game.

ANOTHER WAY

I remember when the bullets flew
and some I loved were counted among the lost.
A father desperate midst depressive gloom
sought respite in the glimmer of a demon's light
and forsaking knowledge of all that love had taught
chose to end a life that once he had begot.

Reeling from the horror of such a monstrous deed
this untempered heart sought refuge in a nether world
midst the island states of a fractured self.
There, hidden from the fearsome glare of an angry god,
salvation's call was but weakly heard for
the clamoring loneliness of the grief and shame.

But life provides no lengthy retreat
from the constancy of its beat
and the fractured center came apart.
Thus the return to that familial spot
where release from hell is bargained sure
at the grinning demon's price.

It was there at the hardest part
when the choice for death drew nigh
that love broke through with a voice I knew,
the cry of heaven to a wounded soul:
"Look through the pain and hold your sway.
There is another way."

And so it is in the midst of our own created hell
God yet calls out to a soul in need,
words resonating with that piece of the divine
cloned into the human spirit on creation's day.

It's not only the sins of the father
that are visited on the children,
but also that spark of the eternal
which breeds love's fire and heeds its call.

There is another way.

Yearnings

The gloom rises from a familial spot,
authored in generations past and
etched into cells love-borne
to worlds which knew it not.

How easily it adapts to each new day,
slowly choking the nascent spirit
with its persistent grasp,
whispering, coaxing, and bullying its way.

What gift is there in tomorrow
when such grayness holds the day,
any freedom from this wearying path,
or respite from the angst and sorrow?

INSOMNIA

Peace, there is no peace
midst the compulsive clatter
of discharging synapses,
anxious thoughts flashing
across my brain,
convulsive ideations
that swamp the soul
and preclude an exit
to the resting place.
Woulda, coulda, shoulda,
my God, what if ....,
a litany without end,
a ceaseless barrage,
no off-ramp from
this interminable intrastate.

October Morning

I push myself through the day
and into the night
and then the morning comes.
And what does Aurora bring?
That familiar, cold stiffness of spirit
which entombs the will
and raises the question "For what?"
from the depths of soul.

Merlins of this present age
ponder the molecular maze
of these tortured depths
and strive to rescore
the endorphin dance,
but who can say what
spark of the divine
can wrest a yes from
the keening spirit and
rouse the reluctant sinew
to purposeful action?

Perhaps a glint of some mystic quest
dooms us to this circadian flow.
Would not Sisyphus agree?
But in touch with that love borne of the rood,
who could adopt this Olympian view?
Beneath it all a voice cries out,
"More, there should be more!"

LOOKING FOR JOY

How did I let it slip away
and allow grimness to seize the day?
The song that beckons I cannot sing,
no flights of fancy on the wing.

Seems I lost that spark of joy
when hell dropped in on a troubled boy,
and all the rest has but touched that spot
where love blows warm and feelings hot,
where glimpses of the divine are gifted brief
and gloom does not filch joy like a thief.

How does it happen that the spirit is set free,
that one's true self can simply be?
One thing I sense as I learn my part,
It's something to do with a grateful heart.

A HILL ABOVE MY HOUSE

There is a hill above my house
blessed by the footfalls of a thousand tribes.
I tarry there from time to time to bask
in the comfort of an ageless presence,
to connect the threads of my life
as yet unwoven into stellar scheme.

It is also a spectral place,
echoing murmurs from a troubled past,
voices aching with choices gone awry.
But here I sense such haunting
is prelude to healing
as severed ties inch together guided
by some mysterious, loving hand.

There is such a force within us,
a yearning that we be whole.
I feel it most upon this hill
special in the autumn evening light
when flaming maples sing of joy,
their leaves in mortal passing.

GETTING THERE

That you could know me
through and through
without the impediments I carry,
so much heavily trafficked debris
borne from youth till now,
wearing away freedom's impulse,
causing hope to flicker like a fading ember.
Ashes, so much is ashes.
O that a spark of life
could course my veins again,
strong through emboldened blood
to cells starved for a quickened pulse.

Choosing life is no mean task.
An idle breath cannot fetch the mark.

At a Distance

Do not come too close,
I am not ready for you.
Disparate parts of me tumble about
in some Brownian milieu
and fail to coalesce
to presentable view.

Do not come too close,
the stress I cannot abide.
These painful collisions play havoc
with my fragile spheres
and trigger still the deepest fears.

Do not come too close,
I find some comfort in our present dance.
Yet the uneasy rhythms
which drive this entropic play
prove a taxing beat by which to sway.

Do not come too close,
the dissonance, I fear, will cease.
Then must I endure the softening.
of your savage gaze,
and taste your meat in length of days.

Do not come too close,
I've learned the footsteps oh too well.
But dare I risk the ingest
of your uncertain feast,
could love's energy
fuse the sundering beast?

FAITH STOPS

After all the time
and all the space,
all the healing
and all the grace,
how did it come to this?

At that first faint-hearted step
when You bid me have faith,
and the next and the next
when your call was the same,
how could I have ever known?

I'm back at the doubting place
troubled again by cares and woes.
But each time I visit
it all seems so new.
How could I have agreed to this?

The depression and the fear
seem too much to bear,
but then you know all about that.
In sight of Calvary high
you breathed many a sigh.

In that fearsome light
my load appears slight
and I pray for the grace to go on.
Bear with me Lord,
I'm trying so hard.

THORN AND FLESH

I have hungered sore for final reprieve
      from an often vexing plaint,
that heaven remove the chafing fetters
      from this aspiring saint.

Rather in the night when sleep is light
      and the demons often stir,
a quiet voice bids me rejoice
      with its tenor oh so sure.

"Those unnerving lows and fearful woes
      which seem a needless mix,
are but a tempering yoke and a healing spoke
      which prove my saving fix."

2

THE COLLIER'S TASK

He descends to the pit
on yet another day
with wisps of a breeze
still fresh in his hair.
Responsibility calls
from the depths of the shaft
where life is cheapened
by the meanness of the task.
We hire him to burn for us,
his heated breath
to warm our hearth
and sustenance.
It's that way
for those we need
merely for a task.

DANCING AT THE FEAST

There are some who come to dance
At the feast of life each day,
And some who choose to watch
While others have their sway.

Still others opt to feed
upon the rhythm and the beat,
while unpracticed steps prove too much
for those with bloodied feet.

But imposters are the ones to scorn,
sidling along with desperate ease,
their meager gestures forsaking inner truth
as fickle judges they seek to please,

when the music stops.

THE SUNDAY SERVICE

Chords resound from another time
and voices pay homage
to some captured reverence
which time has long forgot.
Listeners cling to a fragile hope
the spell will not short be got.

The harmony ends and with it
a brief glimpse of the divine.
Thus does the ritual decline.

The cross which these sonorous
sounds confess becomes,
with them, etched in time,
safely, at a distance, where
bloodied splinters present
no troubling sign.

Trapped in this Sabbath interval
hungering souls do but faintly touch,
that Calvary's work be not too much.

WORD POWER

How few the questing hearts
which find their mark,
undeterred by mouthed words
oft repeated yet
mindless still,
decibelled and cadenced
to capture the will.

Chanted fear, resentment,
un-love for an other,
each forego more care-ful thought,
simplifying life beyond
all true intent,
vexing heaven and earth
with their errant bent.

Whether -can or –crat,
–ist or –ite
comfort is taken in each such role,
freedom thus relinquished
to a menial power,
no truthful tremors
deep felt hour by hour.

IMPULSE

A weapon at hand
in freedom's blessed land
stirs impulsive right
for savage might
to have its way
on any troubling day.

SPIRITUAL WARFARE

A great sadness the fruit of moneyed might,
They who conspire to quench the light,
Broods o'er this blessed land
Where few are they who brave to stand.

Demons evolved to seize this time
Stalk the earth now in their prime,
Binding captured minds and wizened hearts,
Demanding those thus lost refuse their parts.

The light of the world is but a faint glow,
He whose presence once stole the show,
His life now edited by reasonable men
Who praise their work with a great amen.

So we who wither midst the storm,
The feint of heart too much the norm,
Must lay claim our destined roles,
And seek to save our very souls.

The man whose blindness gave way to light,
Brought to his knees after a stubborn fight,
Bids us take up arms against a seasoned foe
Our weapons of the Spirit to bring him low.

With truth and faith as belt and shield,
The sword of God is loathe to yield,
The helmet and breastplate fend off the darts
While the shoes of peace make bold our hearts.

You and I will come through this fight
And best the terror of the night,
Having stood and fought we will not fall,
We will be victors after all.

3

COUPLES

We two are uneasy in the coupling yoke
and at times I chafe at your independent stroke.
We move in sync along the smoother lane,
but the cobbled path can stir a bristling pain.

And when I feel the pull of your unevened pace,
I can respond in kind with a stiffened face.
But to get full measure from our common stride
I must challenge you gently from the other side.

This pain quite sure is of another kind,
and one more difficult to choose I find.
For love's effort requires a fronting gaze,
open and honest, not e'er lackadais.

The test then comes with the next roughened beat,
or the independent strain is once again to meet.
For if love was not practiced before so well,
the journey soon will lose its spell.

FAMILY COURT

Docket 23: Smith vs. Smith.
Docket 24: Jones vs. Jones.
An endless procession,
husband against wife,
child in the lurch,
angst in her eyes,
defiance in his,
and sitting on high,
her wisdom to dispense,
a soft-spoken judge
patient to her task,
striving to have it all make sense.

This scene played out
in a thousand such rooms
brings peace to a troubled land,
or so it would seem.
But the pain goes on
when the gavel comes down
and the costs are not easily borne.
The price is exacted in flesh and blood
and for every such heart-wrenching action
few there are
who leave the Court
with any true satisfaction

How does it start,
this interminable array,
a pledged I do,
a fervent kiss, a moment of bliss.
a child or two, a simmering stew?
So it would seem.
But love's base proves thin
as life cuts in
and the glow fades slowly away.
Anger invades,
steals into the bones,
and hearts are driven at bay.

A Painful Passing

Her quiet dignity belied the
tremors of a troubled soul,
patiently plying her vowed calling.

A feeble voice rose from the ER bed.
"Where are you going?"

In resigned passage
she had borne his fears,
leaching like acid
through denied graces,
etching wounds deep
in the tenderest passages
of her heart.

"I will not leave you" her sure reply.

"Where are you?"
came his follow-up cry.

She had stepped aside to
discuss protocols for
his enfeebled body,
there were none for
for his troubled soul.

"I am here" came
the somewhat weaker reply.

He had protected her from
everything but himself,
declining the fearful return
to Eden's door
where a serpent's spiel
had wrested his manhood
for the price of a pome fruit.

"Don't leave me!"

She had resolved to go,
but it was too late for them now.
Her words were even softer then
as through clenched teeth
they sapped her vital store,
this time a somewhat longer pause
before her feint reply.

"I am here, I will not leave you,
……..now".

LOVE'S BALANCE

I sense our return to the dieing place
Where words collide with meager grace.

We fill the air with opposing parts
And void the space common to our hearts.

The needs of self versus those that bond,
How to keep them in balance and still be fond.

We walk the edge of this slippery slope
And sometimes the best we can do is cope.

This is work to be sure, but of such a kind
Blessings are rife, the toil not to mind.

As we stick together through the difficult parts,
Love will abound in our energized hearts.

4

LABYRINTH

How difficult to find one's way
midst the yoked labyrinth of priest and tribe,
to break the bonds of inured custom
and let the heart its own nectar to imbibe.

Too often we wither in the grasp of the maze
and tire before freedom's final turn,
how loving and persistent must the Spirit be
that bids us the inner voice to discern.

It's a lonely struggle to be sure
and no earthly reward beckons us onward,
merely the gift of one's true self,
free of the conditioning byword.

RESPITE

Midst dappled stillness
gray with wet night fog
we ply the footsteps
of our unexamined lives.

This frightful mist
does but seldom clear
though we shout it down
with chosen clamor and din,
that noise of the daily round
above which the still small voice
is but faintly heard.

What demon curse impels us
along such a hurried highway,
what anxious fears preclude
our exit to a resting spot
to dare heed words
which trickle from the soul like sap
from the spring-struck maple,
words pried from winter's grasp
by the sweetening fires of solitude
to be fused into messages of hope
and purpose for our bone-tired lives?

Time

Don't kill it and
don't fill it,
so what do we do?
It's too short
we pine for more,
it's too long
we wish it by.

Perhaps it is the word
itself which needs to go,
time into time
and out of our lives,
that each moment
becomes real,
grasped to the full.

Then the last will
be the best
and no voice
will say hurry,
let it pass,
or more,
I need more!

WINTER RAIN

This rain's smell is not so sweet
and its guttered rivulets flow
with an icy sheen.
Shoulders hunch at the feel
of its gelid drops
and the taste of their harsh coldness
numbs the innermost workings
of the imagining place.
It is winter and the heart listens
for the gentler sound
of the summer rain.

THE HEALING SEA

The sea lies still
and I cast upon it the cares
of a life lived full.
Immersed in its tendrillar grasp,
the gentle sweep of each muted crest
slides inward
and softens the blows
of a care-less world.
And then, on the ebb,
the refuse of grief and pain
is loosed from its moorings
to slowly seep through each pore
and slide back into the timeless deep.

5

CHOICES (I)

I drift upon a restless sea
bereft of a sense of destiny,
or so the world would have it be.
But 'neath the surface I live more free
and a deeper truth is known to me.
I choose my place in eternity

CHOICES (II)

There comes a time
when the heart well knows
that choices are not lightly taken,
when the stakes are high
to answer the cry
of a world so sadly shaken.

It is here that the call
must be carefully weighed
and life's baggage left by the door,
for the voice that is heard
is quite soon deterred
if the self be the focus more.

But if one can choose
to enter the pain
and bear the load ever longer,
that heart will know
that it can grow
and prove so much the stronger.

When the clarion cry
then sounds once again
with an urgency yet more compelling,
the tempered heart will respond well
to the call and its spell
and that life will be more for the telling.

CHOICES (III)

Either/or, the options plain and smooth,
If life be so simple
Why fear a wrongful move?

Either/or, each a different path,
But choosing one
Ordains its aftermath.

Either/or, the choice is surely mine,
It is freedom sure,
But of a vexing kind.

Either/or, God bids me choose,
And with His all-forgiving love
I cannot lose.

6

SPACE/TIME

Imagine time
no time to measure,
and space
no object to view.
Requires a link with the eternal
some would say.

Yet takes a bare moment
to enter such space,
this moment, this space,
the space within,
where emptiness is fecund and
from which all manifestation flows,
the light therein a purposeful beam,
gift of the Spirit
at matter's amazing birth.

Was not such a pregnant gleam
creation's prize for Einstein's pause
when first he saw the two as one,
space and time, each born in the
same sudden flash, of necessity bound?
Deepest thought conjured such a truth
that thought itself now yearns to grasp
as Newton's familiar certainty
proves but prelude to mystery
and seeming subjective flair.

Creation is seen anew
since that patent man
grasped the light,
the finger of God tracing
ever more difficult code,
speaking to us of relativity,
of probability, of possibility,
a chaotic universe unfolding
in ordered measure through time,
all taking vision to decipher,
connection with a deeper truth
beyond the bent of self-limiting mind,
of culture and belief set to have their way.

Did not Galileo's find also
require release from current thought
and egregious denial
proved non-sense in history's clear sight?
And so with Darwin and evolution's fate,
how we continue to resist,
even at this late date!

ENTANGLEMENT

A simple word but layered deep
with strangeness beyond the zen
of fly-trapped web or Medusan hair,
trysting lovers or bald untruths,
of these we have a basic ken.

Now comes the cosmic seer,
versed in realms of symbolic code,
speaking to us of bits of light
mystically paired thru time and space,
each complicit in the other's mode.

But does not creation's every word
go forth to touch a receptive ear,
stirring a seeking spirit into
a moment's sudden trance,
a certain stillness required to hear?

HALF-LIFE

Halfway to the door and half again,
ever onward yet shy of the mark.
We know the math as that particle unseen,
its decay set in practiced rite.

And so if one's life be seen in half,
as nothing but a stonéd path.
It is a measure of hell to be sure
for eternity cannot bring its end.

Yet we somehow trust in death's feared door
to take a life in half and make it whole,
or in oblivion's quick fix
to erase the pain of a self-filled world.

This hoped for voiding of creation's aim
belies a deeper truth beyond the grave,
the hound of heaven's relentless love
ever disturbs such vainly sought repose.

THE BIG BANG

The motes of time
drift through focused light,
glimpsing that infant day
when tiny bits
first stretched
to flex their might.

The Lord of the Dance
had set them free
with barely a hint
of their destiny.

Who could have thought
what that would be?

Certainly not me.

The heavens declare the glory of God,
    the skies proclaim the work of his hands.
Day after day they pour forth speech;
    night after night they display knowledge.
There is no speech or language
    where their voice is not heard.
Their voice goes out into all the earth,
    their words to the ends of the world.
                Psalm 19: 1-4

THE ATOMS' TALE

I began with that first flash of light
heeding the creator's command,
birthed within the weightiest
of implausible specks,
affixed to the arrow
of space/time,
and shot into the future
for the ride of my life.
Now, the very atoms
which brought me to consciousness
bear the most wondrous of tales.

They sing of quarks and strings
and other things,
a concoction of strange particles
and entangled forces
in a charmed and colored milieu,
all rising from the heat
of that first seminal moment
to cool and coalesce,
birthing the progenitor of their race,
the star seed hydrogen.

It was gravity burst its bounds
within that pinhead cauldron
spewing the universe forth,
gravity too then herding
those tiny seeds together,
forcing paired fusion
into helium atoms
and setting the stars ablaze,
their light a messenger
bearing the atoms' tale.

The atoms' language is light itself,
its alphabet and syntax now
deciphered to read their story
in a photon's measure,
the electron shield of each atom
emitting spikes of quantized light,
different, one from another,
each with its own fingerprint
recording its journey
thru space and time.

A rainbow's arc provides but a glimpse
of this light's informing power
observed through telescope eyes
attuned to its alphabet range,
radio waves thru the visible zone
to ultraviolet rays and beyond,
each atom singly or molecule bound
usurping its own photonic array
to tell it's tale.

It is such light that sings
of beryllium and carbon,
oxygen and silicon, iron and more,
their fusion with helium and lesser bits,
or fission in a billion degree astral furnace
to create the full complement of stellar progeny,
ninety two of these atomic wunderkind
shed from parental stars in layers,
like the skin of an onion,
or blown into the universe by exploding novas
with luminous displays outshining
the light of a hundred million suns.

It is light reveals these
stardust components
bonding one with another
and gravity-powered merger
into planets, the incubators of life;
carbon's molecular unions with
hydrogen, nitrogen and oxygen
in simple array,
structured beginnings
to the stuff of life,
proteins and DNA,
perhaps hitching a ride
on some distant comet
to begin my assembly,
one fine planet earth day.

It is light beaming
from countless stars
in numberless galaxies
that spins this epic tale,
billions of years in its telling
mere decades in our understanding,
the atoms evincing a creativity
spawned with that first light
heeding the creator's command,
forging a universe of
nested components in
synergy mode,
their mission:
 life, its continuous evolution,
 and story told.

                    P

              O   R
       T
          E
                          Y

                                      N

ENTROPY

Disorder so much
the order of each day,
despite the seeming
magic of feng shui.

It's a more active force
must come to play
should the arrow of time
not hold its sway.

POETRY

I step out onto
that difficult plane
where words struggle
to surface through
a labyrinthine milieu,
sometimes coalescing
in holy alliance
but often in entropic
display of scattered
thoughts and feelings.

It is only when the
disciplined hand
grasps the discordant
threads and moves them
through the hard place
to the other side of creation
that the latent message
assumes rhapsodic form,
startling the spirit
with its sudden song.

7

VINCENT'S LIGHT

Vincent glimpsed the star-filled night
with its darkness and its light
the polarities of his own madness,
challenging mind and canvas
to reveal the intensity of his sight.

His was a rare gift to absorb so
readily the subtle machinations of light,
discerning its truth as it passed
from the brilliance of the daytime hour
to a twinkling presence in the nighttime sky.

Who could see Vincent's *Starry Night*
and not be stirred by its view of the heavens
with its giant corpuscles and waves of light
exploding as if from the Creator's hand,
revelations of such power, goodness and delight?

Vincent succumbed to the darkness,
but his legacy, his gift to the world,
his light captured with paint and brush,
tells us so much of life, of who we are,
and who we are called to be.

THE EGRET

The egret stalks its prey
in a sea of grass
rich with the flow
of a tidal rush,
the world at work
this quiet morning,
its myriad components
faithful to their task,
guidance breathed
through remnants
of a violent birth
organized by some
mysterious power
specific to each
atom, creature and star,
yet unified to direct
a wondrous whole,
life in its richness
revealed in a moment's
glimpse of the world at hand.

ANGELS

It is the rustle of
lithesome wings
which oft disturbs my spirit
when I least expect it,
reminding me that
angelic hosts
reside not solely
on the heads of pins,
but move with
a fluttering grace
through the portals
of the soul,
loosing the
carapaced vapors
which vitiate hope,
peace and joy.

I think they laugh
a lot as well,
something we humans
need more to do,
for it's laughter which
fuels their winged work,
pulsing vibrations
sometimes felt in those
quiet moments when
the spirit is stirred
long enough for us
to catch a glimpse of
their constant view,
the face of the divine.

MOMENTS

How does it happen
that at times the wolfen door
is barred and I can sit
in the reflection of a
mystical moment
and know
that all is right
within and about me?

How does it happen
that at times fear is kept
under proper choke
and cannot steal the bliss
of a moment's wake,
that the deepest place
is visited wherein the seed
of joy is sown?

How does it happen
that at times you and I
can catch those moments
when the songs get sung
and the icy loneliness
of our brief strut
is tempered by the glow
of a mutual spell?

How does it happen
that at times a glimpse
of the eternal
becomes our view,
a sense of oneness
with creation,
and the wonder of it all
becomes our greatest delight?

Who writes the script for
such a far-fetched play,
who gets the parts?

ACKNOWLEDGEMENTS

Special thanks to:

My wife, Ann, for her constant support during my 20+ years of writing poetry, for her comments and editing helps, and her strong encouragement for me to publish this book.

Lynne Nelson for her help with the editing and selection of my poems, for her strong encouragement to publish them, and for her writing the description of this book which appears on the back cover.

Marie Edmeades who read many of my poems, created the internal artwork and was instrumental in choosing the title.

Joan Semenuk who included several of the poems in her daily spiritual meditations provided *via* the internet.

Richard Zboray who recommended needed changes in my use of antiquated words and provided thoughtful questions regarding the wording and titles of various poems.

Carol Tessman, Sally Bailey, Maurice and Beatty Raymond, and Alex and Krystyna Schenker who listened to my readings and were very supportive at different times during the gestation period for this book.

Emma Blanch, the editor of *Twilight Ending, A Literary Journal*, for her early mentoring and inclusion of three of my poems in 1996-7 editions.

Edwards Brothers Malloy
Thorofare, NJ USA
March 31, 2015